BECAUSE *of* GRÁCIA

A FILM AND FAITH LEADER'S GUIDE
THEME I: PRACTICING FRIENDSHIP

NASHVILLE

Dexterity, LLC
604 Magnolia Lane
Nashville, TN 37211
Copyright © 2017

All rights reserved. Except as permitted by the US Copyright Act of 1976, no part of this book may be reproduced, distributed, or transmitted without prior written permission from the publisher. For information, please contact info@dexteritycollective.co.

The author gratefully acknowledges the photography of Nick Arnold and Five Stones

Films for making available much of the photography/still shots used in the publication of this work. All rights reserved to Nick Arnold/Five Stones Films. Further and additional use requires permission of the copyright holder: Five Stones Films. All works of Nick Arnold under hire by Five Stones Films are works made for hire and are the exclusive property of Five Stones Films. All rights reserved.

First edition: 2017 10 9 8 7 6 5 4 3 2 1

Printed in the United States of America.

ISBN: 978-1-947297-06-7 (trade paper) ISBN: 978-1-947297-07-4 (ebook)

Book design by Sarah Siegand Designs and Brian Kannard. Cover design by Trent Design, Inc.

All scripture quotations, unless otherwise noted, are taken from THE HOLY BIBLE, NEW INTERNATIONAL VERSION®, NIV® Copyright © 1973, 1978, 1984, 2011 by Biblica, Inc.® Used by permission. All rights reserved worldwide.

*With great power the apostles continued to testify
to the resurrection of the Lord Jesus. And God's grace
was so powerfully at work in them all that there were
no needy persons among them.*
Acts 4:33-34

TABLE OF CONTENTS

A Word from the Director..xv

Introduction..xvii

Theme I: Practicing Friendship

THEME I: PRACTICING FRIENDSHIP INTRODUCTION............... 20

CONVERSATION 1: WHY DO WE FALL IN LOVE? 22
Created for Relationship

CONVERSATION 2: WHAT ABOUT OUR BODIES? 34
God's Design for Sexuality

CONVERSATION 3: HOW DO YOU GROW TRUE 46
FRIENDSHIP?
Healthy Dating 101

About the Authors..55

A WORD
FROM THE DIRECTOR

In 2001 I wrote a play called *G Factor*, which followed a young man named Chase Morgan going through his senior year of high school with his best friend, OB. I started out with one simple scene: Chase in his bedroom trying to get up the nerve to call a new student and ask her out on a date. Chase was an unlikely protagonist, an undercover Christian unsure of how to fit into the world around him.

TOM SIMES

Inexplicably, the play was a big success, and we sold out 6 or 7 nights in a row. For years I thought about Chase as I watched young Christians walking through the door of my public school classroom with lack of confidence in their identities and the fear that someone might discover who they really were and what they believed.

In 2013 I rewrote the story as a screenplay, and during summer 2014 I shot the entire film as a rough cut at the same high school where I was teaching. The story went through some changes—a new beginning and a different ending—but what remained the same were the timely themes of chastity, courtship, sanctity of life, and freedom of speech.

I can't tell you how excited I am that Chris and Michelle have created this practical and highly relevant curriculum for students and leaders. The materials are imaginative and comprehensive, faithful to both the film and to God. Young people working through this resource together will be challenged and encouraged in their faith and reassured in making godly decisions about their sexuality.

My sincere prayer is that the *Because of Grácia* curriculum draws everyone who uses it into a deeper relationship with our Lord and Savior Jesus Christ, and that it helps them find their voice and their confidence the same way Chase Morgan does.

Sincerely,

Tom Simes
writer, director, producer
Because of Grácia

BECAUSE of GRÁCIA

LEADER GUIDE
INTRODUCTION

Becoming a Christian is a beginning followed by a long growth process. People call it *discipleship*, bringing to mind the image of disciples following a master wherever he goes, learning from everything he says and does amid the actions, choices, and relationships of daily life.

This is a discipleship curriculum. Its goal is to shape the real lives of young people as we examine three crucial, practical topics: love and dating, teen pregnancy and abortion, and the expression of Christian faith to the world. The themes are not easy ones. They involve a narrow road and a high calling. They require the communication of high expectations and the assurance of high support. In theological terms, we might say they require an appreciation of both Law ("This is the right thing to do and this is the wrong thing") and Grace ("If you did the wrong thing, there is a way to start over").

Which brings us to *Because of Grácia*. Here is a movie that dramatizes high ideals for the Christian life while treating mercifully those who fail to attain them. The grace in the phrase "because of grace" actually works in two directions at once. Grace isn't only the gift of mercy when we fail, but also the empowerment to live in truth and light. Grace isn't only the forgiveness of sins past, present, and future, but also the transfer from one kingdom to another in which we actually sin less by the power of that kingdom's resurrected King.

In this curriculum we are affirming that, because of God's amazing, pursuing, empowering grace, young people can live in a new way. "We are grateful to you for partnering with us in ministry, whether you are leading students through one or all three of the related theme guides—Practicing Friendship, Choosing Life, and Voicing Faith."

HOW TO USE THIS LEADER GUIDE

This 3-week leader guide for the *Because of Grácia* curriculum has been created to be as interactive, relevant, functional, and flexible a group resource as possible for you and your students. In it, you will find compelling learning games, movie clips, Scripture studies, and video testimonies matched with the 3 topical "conversations" of the guide. In-depth discussion questions form the heart of the process, helping students learn from each other, their mentors, and their own perceptions and experiences.

We recommend that leaders look over the "Session at a Glance" summaries ahead of time and choose the activities best suited to the interests, maturity levels, and time constraints of their group for any given meeting. "Prep" sections remind you in a concise way of the steps and materials that should be completed ahead of each session as well. Throughout each session, the leader's scripted remarks **are clearly marked in bold**.

Video resources
To get the greatest benefit from this resource, we recommend that a group views *Because of Grácia* in its entirety before beginning

this study—either in the theater or via licensed streaming or DVD presentation at a group "movie night." Such an event (complete with popcorn and sodas) can be an excellent way of winning hearts for the subsequent learning process. It will also prepare participants to engage with confidence the issues, characters, and storylines of the film, which the curriculum builds upon through selected movie clips and narrative references.

The movie clips are available in two places: both the official "Resources page" on the *Because of Grácia* website or, by special request, on DVD. As you travel through each of the 9 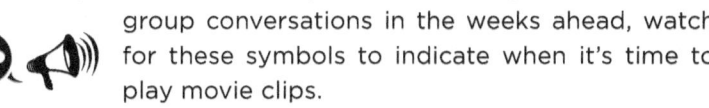 group conversations in the weeks ahead, watch for these symbols to indicate when it's time to play movie clips.

The other video resource provided by the curriculum is a series of topic-linked testimonies from the film's actors and others. There is typically one testimony per group session. Groups will be able to access these in the same location as the movie clips.

Print resources

Participants in the group conversations will benefit from having their student guides, which contain material to support the session's activities. To access the curriculum website for video clips and additional resources go to **http://www.becauseofgracia.com/resources.** We will remind you in the "Prep" sections if you need to access and/or print out these resources ahead of time.

Timing

Group sessions are designed be completed in 60–90 minutes, depending on the depth of discussion pursued and the degree to which the final "Carry It Out" application activities are undertaken. Typically, the material before that point requires an hour and the

"Carry it Out" activity extends into extra time. Groups that meet multiple times in a week may also wish to divide up one session between two meetings—and you may do this in whatever way works for you. We have designed this curriculum to be flexible and adaptable to many kinds of classrooms, so feel free to organize the sessions in the manner that seems right for your unique group setting.

Outside guests

One conversation in this guide includes an "Intergenerational Sidebar"—a set of questions to pose to a visiting guest from another generation, in order to provide opportunity for your participants to benefit from the larger wisdom of the body of Christ. That will take some prior planning to arrange, possibly as early as the initial film screening. You may wish to invite your guest to multiple sessions, but we have only framed formal involvement one time in each of the three main themes.

HOW TO USE THE STUDENT GUIDE

The essential second curriculum resource that accompanies the group-oriented leader guide is the individual student guide. This book is a unique hybrid resource that includes both "Group Session" and "Paired Session" learning content. Every person in your group will benefit from having his or her own copy (both students and leaders).

The group session portions of the student guide support the group learning process by providing activity instructions and discussion questions. Interspersed among the group-oriented material are the unique paired session segments: 5 days of take-home readings for each of the 9 group conversations, for a total of 45 days of purposeful spiritual growth. These segments are part devotional, part journal, part conversation starter. Daily entries are designed for students to travel through with a matched "conversation partner"—likely a peer from the same group. You will be instrumental in making sure that every student has a partner for these paired sessions, and considering the sensitive nature of this material, we suggest you group students together thoughtfully and prayerfully.

As we designed the paired sessions, we wanted to communicate to young Christians that discipleship is best pursued with others—something enjoyable and interactive, not a solitary endeavor. Likewise, we want to inspire and equip young people to "walk the walk and talk the talk" in a vibrant way, as Jesus did in his earthly ministry. We hope your students will find the time they spend with their conversation partner both enjoyable and spiritually challenging.

Ideally, group leaders will also participate in the 45-day paired sessions, perhaps with a spouse or co-leader, in order to track with the learning of students and better answer questions that arise from the material.

In situations where even greater accountability is needed, or when there is an uneven numbers of suitable partners, the paired session process can also be undertaken by a triad or small group. Each paired session is designed to take 20–30 minutes, in addition to optional application activities that keep students thinking as they go about their weeks.

THEME 1

Practicing Friendship

Practicing Friendship
INTRODUCTION

If someone asked, "What is *Because of Grácia* about, in a single word?" the answer would be *friendship*. That includes friendship based on respectful, mutually empowering companionship; friendship that intensifies into passion and goes astray; and friendship that reaches out to help those in trouble. The goal of this first theme is to empower participants for the first and last kind of true friendship and to help them avoid the snares of the wandering-astray kind.

There is a risk involved in calling young people to high ideals in a sensitive area of life. One desires to make a strong appeal for righteousness, but one doesn't want to condemn or discourage those who know that their actions tend to go in the opposite direction. How can we deal with this tension? How can we answer difficult questions and provide valuable answers to students who deserve knowledge *and* wisdom when it comes to the difficult terrain of friendship and sexuality? We hope that amid this theme's group sessions and partnered conversations, students will learn how the need for relationship is part of our essential nature as beings made in the image of God—and that the physical aspects of relationship, in proper alignment with God's will, can be holy and good.

Here are some approaches that may be useful as you tackle these difficult conversations with your students. We don't expect leaders to cover all these matters in the group session, but we do

want to outline some helpful concepts and perspectives for when questions are asked:
- Sexuality is beautiful and complex. God knows all about it and approves of its pleasures and delights since he designed it.
- Because sexual experience is powerfully bonding, it should be used to create bonds established and safeguarded by a marriage covenant—especially since it has the potential to generate new life.
- Sexual drive is powerful. It can run away with our decision-making processes. We might make choices in the heat of the moment that we would not have made otherwise.
- Because our Lord is Forgiver, Deliverer, and Healer, there is restoration from sexual sin, sexual bondage, and sexual wounding of all kind.

Jesus maintained an ideal balance between the invitation to holiness and the expression of loving forgiveness for those who knew they had not been holy. He had the reputation of being a friend to sinners, even as he issued forceful calls to the people of his time to repent of sin. Some of the sinners who wanted to be near him were actually willing to risk public shame if only to be able to properly express their love and admiration for him and the new beginning he offered (take, for example, the woman who anointed him with perfume at a certain dinner party).

We encourage leaders using this guide to hold up the "high support, high expectations" stance of Jesus as their ideal in teaching this material. As Jesus himself said to a vulnerable heart in John 8:11, "Neither do I condemn you...Go now and leave your life of sin."

CONVERSATION 1
WHY DO WE FALL IN LOVE?
CREATED FOR RELATIONSHIP

KEY INSIGHT

>>> We are created for relationship—to love and to be loved. God is our first love, and we are to love others as well.

AT A GLANCE

SET THE STAGE
- A Perfect Love Story
- Honey, Do You Love Me?

REEL TO REAL
- Chase falling for Grace
- The phone call
- What came of it

ENGAGE THE WORD
- Genesis 2:4–25: The first relationships

REPORT FROM THE FRONTLINES
- Brett Simes (OB) on relationship

CARRY IT OUT
- Introducing students to their conversation partners

PREP

SET THE STAGE: From the *Because of Grácia* Resources website, print a copy of "A Perfect Love Story" (1 copy per group leader).

REEL TO REAL / REPORT FROM THE FRONTLINES: Cue up the session's three movie clips and the video testimony for presentation.

ENGAGE THE WORD: From the *Because of Grácia* Resources website, print the "Genesis 2 Improv" script (1 copy per group leader).

CARRY IT OUT: We recommend you prayerfully create a matched list of student guide conversation partners ahead of time and keep it on hand.

 SET THE STAGE

If you have more than an hour for your session, try both activities. Otherwise, choose one of the two.

 A Perfect Love Story

LEADER: Why do people fall in love? We want to use your creativity today to arrive at a possible answer.

Use the resource you printed from the curriculum website to create wacky love stories with session participants in groups of 25-30.

First, go through the blanks of the story one by one and ask for volunteers to contribute the kind of word needed in each case. The narrative begins: *"Once there was a* [type of person] *named* [man's name] *who fell in love with a* [type of person] *named* [woman's name]. *It was a match made in* [place name]. Ask your group, "Give me a type of person. Now give me a man's name," and so on. Do this without reading any of the actual narrative yet.

Next, once all the blanks are filled in, read the story to the group from start to finish. Participants will be interested to see how their suggested words play out in context.

Once the laughter has died down, discuss the following as a group:

Discuss

- What are the essential elements of a classic love story?
- We all want relationship, right? Then why are relationships so difficult?

2 Honey, Do You Love Me?

Choose 2 volunteers to demonstrate this. The object of this game is simple: to keep a straight face. Along with fun and mingling, the teaching objective is to encourage participants to think about the challenge of reaching out for relationship.

Gather 20–30 people in a circle with an even mix of guys and girls. (If your group is large, make multiple circles with an adult leading each one.) Choose someone to be "it." That person needs to approach a member of the opposite sex and ask this question: "Honey, do you love me?" The person being asked needs to make eye contact and answer, "Honey, I love you, but I just can't smile"—without smiling. If they smile, they become the new "it." If they are successful in not smiling, the existing "it" continues around the circle, asking others. The adult game leader is the judge of whether a person has smiled or not.

Play for at least 5 minutes. It takes a lot of willpower to keep a straight face in this game, but if anyone happens to get stuck in the middle for too long as "it," set a limit of 5 rounds before choosing another person to take their place.

If the leader helps set a tone of lighthearted fun rather than serious competition, the game will be safer for participants' feelings. That said, leaders should assess ahead of time whether their particular group is too vulnerable or unfamiliar with one another to play this game.

Discuss

- What does it feel like to be the question-asker in this game? Why does it feel awkward?
- What does it feel like to be the question-answerer?
- Which role would you rather play? Why?
- Are there male-female differences in this game? Is one of the roles more comfortable for males and one of the roles more comfortable for females?
- Would you rather: fall in love with someone you couldn't have, or have someone you didn't like fall in love with you?

Note to Leader: We are using the term love *without much examination at this point. We'll continue to shape that term throughout the sessions, moving from the senses of* crush *and* infatuation, *through* desire, *to the self-giving* agape *love that Christ has modeled.*

REEL TO REAL

LEADER: Today's movie clips illustrate how complicated—and sometimes awkward—love and relationships can be.

1. Chase falling for Grace *(2:08)*

- How can you tell Chase is falling for Grace? What effect is she having on him?
- Why are we drawn to certain people? Is it a simple thing or a complicated thing?
- Why is it so hard for Chase to take the initiative to get to know Grácia? What is the "pressure" he's feeling? What is he afraid of?

LEADER: Let's see what happens as Chase tries again.

2. The phone call *(2:19)*

- Can you relate to Chase's experience in this situation? Is it true to life?

26 | BECAUSE OF GRÁCIA **LEADER GUIDE**

- Is awkwardness and nervousness with someone we're attracted to more of a guy thing or more a girl thing? Do girls show nervousness in different ways than guys do?

- What do we want most from someone we admire?

3. What came of it *(0:56)*

- Do Chase and Grácia feel the same way about each other?

- Why isn't Grácia afraid to ask Chase to meet up somewhere?

- How is Chase feeling after the phone call?

 ENGAGE THE WORD

LEADER: Have we gotten any closer to an answer to today's session title—*Why do we fall in love?* [Take some suggestions.] **It's an interesting expression, "falling in love." Why don't we call it "stepping in love" or "sprouting in love" or "climbing in love"? Why "falling"? Is this "falling" a good aspect of being human or a not-good aspect? Why couldn't relationships between people just be simple and logical? Why are we driven by such powerful need and held back by such powerful fear? Let's take a look at the founding story of humankind, as told by Genesis 2, and see what light it sheds on the matter.**

Present a condensed reading of Genesis 2 accompanied by spontaneous dramatic improvisation, using the script from the *Because of Grácia* website. The idea with this activity is to use creativity and fun to engage students' imaginations with the actual details of the biblical story rather than allowing them to "glaze over" as soon as a Bible is being read. The activity can involve the whole group at once (lower participation, greater focus) or in smaller groups of 20–30 (higher participation, greater chaos).

Begin by taking volunteers to play the following roles:
- 3 individuals acting and speaking simultaneously to play the part of God (an arrangement similar to the terms of Genesis 18)
- Assorted beasts and birds (3-5 people)
- Adam
- Eve
- A river
- 4 trees

Next, read the story according to the segments in the printout, leaving enough time between each segment (even up to a minute) for the relevant action to occur onstage. Pauses for actions are marked in the script with bracketed double lines [===].

Actors are to act out the action they hear as the narrator reads and pauses. When speech occurs in the narrative, actors should repeat the lines fed to them by the narrator.

The script begins, *When the Lord God made the earth and the heavens, the Lord God formed the man from the dust of the ground* [===]. *And he breathed into his nostrils the breath of life* [===], *and the man became a living being* [===]...

LEADER: The creation account of Genesis 1 says over and over again that God thought his creation was good. Genesis 2 is the first time in the Bible that something is called "not good." What was that thing? [Take suggestions.] **Yes, it's when the man is alone. In verse 18, God says, "It is not good for the man to be alone."**

Discuss

- Why isn't it good to be alone?
- Wasn't it enough for Adam to have God as a friend?

LEADER: God says he will make a partner, a "helper" for the man. Elsewhere in the Bible, God himself is called a helper, using the same Hebrew word.

Adam responds with delight in what is the first quoted human speech in the Bible. Do you remember what he said? [Take examples.]

Discuss

- What does it say about God that he recognizes Adam's need for companionship with someone similar to Adam?
- What do you think it means that woman was "taken out of man"?
- Does this story explain why we fall in love?

LEADER: We don't have time today to act out what happens next in the story, so I'll summarize it. At the end of Genesis 2, it says, "Adam and his wife were both naked, and they felt no shame." In other words, they had nothing to hide—nothing to worry about in front of each other.

But then they disobeyed God by eating from the forbidden Tree of Knowledge of Good and Evil, and things changed. The text says, "Then the eyes of both of them were opened, and they realized they were naked; so they sewed fig leaves together and made coverings for themselves" (Genesis 3:7).

They covered themselves to keep themselves safe physically, but also emotionally. They began to hide their vulnerability from one another. And they also hid from God among the trees of the garden. When God found them, the first thing they did was throw around blame for what had happened. God told them that their relationship—which had already taken a serious turn for the worse—was going to become even more troubled as a result.

It is important that we appreciate the good, profound, God-given need that we have for one another as men and women—the need not to be alone but to be in mutually helpful and delightful partnerships together. At the same time, we must appreciate that this need has been disturbed by the selfishness and shame that flow from the entry of sin into the world. This explains both why we fall in love and why the falling can be so awkward and painful.

Human beings' broken relationship with God has a deep effect on our relationships. What should we do about this? Well, if the breaking of our relationship with God resulted in troubled relationships with each other, then maybe the healing of our relationship with God can lead to renewed relationships with each other.

Note to Leader: This session provides a natural opportunity to talk about reconciling with God through Jesus, if there are those present who have never considered such a thing. Following up on the theme of our deep need for relationship in general, you might speak of what Jesus does for our relationship with God: He absorbs the cost of our rebellion; he puts God's forgiveness into force in our lives; he restores relational peace with God; and he transforms our desire to hide from God into a desire to come to him and lovingly obey him as our Father.

<u>**LEADER:**</u> **We need to be aware that if we don't pay attention to our broken relationship with God, then we may try to fill that ultimate relational need with less-than-ultimate relationships. We may try to use others to fulfill something in us that only God can truly fulfill.**

 # PRAYER

Lead the group in a prayer of dedication or rededication to intimate relationship with God before all others.

REPORT FROM THE FRONTLINES

On the *Because of Grácia* Resources website, watch Brett Simes, who plays the character of OB in the film, talk about amazement at the opposite sex, our need for relationship, and our need for God. (Clip is 4:13.)

LEADER: Though we can learn a lot from each other during our group sessions, why stop there? In a few minutes, I will be assigning each of you a conversation partner, with whom you can continue this discussion throughout the week. In your student guide, you have everything you need to carry on a study of this theme addressed by *Because of Grácia*. Over the next 3 weeks, you and your conversation partner have an awesome opportunity to grow as you read God's Word together, ask and answer hard questions, and reflect upon how to turn what we're talking about into action.

CARRY IT OUT
Conversation Partners

Match students with conversation partners, with whom they will journey through the paired sessions over the next 3 weeks. Students can find a place to sit together and make plans for how they will schedule and conduct their paired sessions. Try to reserve enough time for them to discuss the entry for Week 1, Day 1 ("Longing for God").

CONVERSATION 2
WHAT ABOUT OUR BODIES?
GOD'S DESIGN FOR SEXUALITY

KEY INSIGHT

>>> Honoring God and telling the truth with our bodies means saving the bonding, life-generating intimacies of sexuality for the context of a marriage relationship.

AT A GLANCE

SET THE STAGE
- Knowing by Touch
- Blind Charades
- Sticky Contest

REEL TO REAL
- Bobbi and Jesse home alone
- At the tracks and afterward
- Grace tells her story

ENGAGE THE WORD
- John 8:1–11: The woman caught in adultery

REPORT FROM THE FRONTLINES
- Louisa Wendorff (Josie) on physical attraction

CARRY IT OUT
- Popularize Chastity

> # PREP
>
> ***SET THE STAGE:*** Have on hand a blindfold, a roll of duct tape, and a pair of scissors.
>
> ***REEL TO REAL / REPORT FROM THE FRONTLINES:*** Cue up the session's three movie clips and video testimony for presentation.
>
> ***ENGAGE THE WORD:*** Bookmark the session's main text (John 8:1–11).

 # SET THE STAGE

The introductory activities for this session get participants thinking about the significance of our physical bodies: how our physical selves are part of our identity, our communication, and our way of knowing others. Try as many as fit your time frame, but we recommend Sticky Contest if you only have time for one.

 Knowing by Touch

Choose a girl from the group to wear a blindfold. Next, ask a handful of boys to line up facing her. Then ask her to blindly touch their heads, hands, and feet—nothing else. See if she can name the boys in the lineup based upon her blind touch. Only choose volunteers for the lineup who won't be embarrassed by being identified according to their physical features.

Discuss

- Would you agree that we are our bodies? Or are we *more* than our bodies?

- What can you know about someone based on their body? What can't you know about them?

2 Blind Charades

LEADER: Helen Keller was a woman who lost the ability to see and hear at a young age, but she was very intelligent and became a renowned speaker and author. Her childhood teacher developed a communication system with her that involved presenting sign language by touch in the palm of Helen's hand. We're going to find out how easy it is to communicate with a method like that.

Choose 2 volunteers to demonstrate this activity in front of the whole group.

Blindfold the guesser in the game. The communicator has to help the guesser guess the chosen words and phrases through touch only—no talking or sound effects. For example, to communicate the word hat, you might make your hands into a hat on the person's head; to communicate cold, you might rub the person's shoulders as though to warm them up or blow on their arm; to communicate Jesus, you might press the person's palms and feet in sequence.

Sample words for the game:
- hat
- Jesus
- dancing
- basketball
- mouse
- cold
- apple
- music
- baseball
- moustache
- jump
- painting
- lion

A person is vulnerable when blindfolded. Choose only a trustworthy communicator for this game and be very clear about the rules: no pain, no surprises. The communicator needs to treat the guesser as one would treat a seeing- and hearing-impaired person—with great respect and care.

After the demonstration, let everyone in the room try the same challenge briefly with the person beside them. (Just ask one partner to close their eyes). Tell the signing partner to choose a food in their mind and try to communicate that choice using only touch.

Discuss

- How easy is it to communicate through touch? What kinds of things does touch communicate well? What is harder to communicate with touch?

LEADER: We don't always recognize what we are really saying, or trying to say, with our bodies. And we don't always understand what someone else is saying, or meaning to say. What are some of the things we can say with our bodies? [Take suggestions]

That brings us to the subject of sexuality. You knew we'd get there sooner or later! Sex is a special means of communication between 2 people. Within God's design, sex says, "You are not alone. We belong together as one. You can trust me to cherish every part of you. You don't need to fear me, and you don't need to be ashamed of yourself in front of me. I will love and protect you for your lifetime, no matter what happens." Sex also says, "Our communion must remain and grow for our whole lives. It's so special, we can create a new human being that brings

who we are together, literally, into one flesh. We are ready to provide a committed, permanent home for this being. We have already established it."

Whether we know it or not, sex between 2 people says all of this—or it *should* say all of this. If sex doesn't express these things, it could be saying other things—such as, "I don't need to know anything more about you; I don't care about your future; you are only important to me right now." Sex should tell God's truth. When we have sex and aren't expressing God's truth at the same time, we can damage others and ourselves.

3 Sticky Contest

Ask for 3 volunteers to compete in a sticky contest, where the player with the stickiest tape bond wins. Begin with 2 large pieces of duct tape, and hand them to volunteer A. Tell volunteer A to stick the pieces together; then ask volunteer B to try to separate them. Next, take 2 fresh pieces of tape and stick them once on your clothes, once on the floor, and once on the sole of your shoe. Then hand them over to volunteer C to stick together. Can volunteer B separate them more easily?

Discuss

- Was this a fair contest?
- Which pieces of tape were easier to pull apart? Why?

- If the pieces of tape are human beings and the stickiness is the strength of the bond between them, what might this demonstration show?
- Where does this demonstration fall short in providing an image of sexual bonding and its results?

LEADER: God has created sexuality with a tremendous bonding power. It is important that we use that power in the context of a lifelong, committed relationship—that is, in marriage—where it can do the good work it is designed to do. That strong bond will be necessary not only to hold together 2 adults in covenant through a long and challenging life journey, but also to provide a stable home that many other people can rely on, including the children created by that bond.

This is not to say there can be no healing of our sexual selves once we have diminished that bonding power through careless sexuality. There is more redemption possible for people than for duct tape! But why go through that wounding, suffering, and healing if you don't have to? Sure, broken bones can heal, but that is no reason to step in front of a moving car.

In today's movie clips, we are going to see Bobbi and Jesse explore the power of sexual communication before they are ready to tell the full truth with it. And we are going to hear Grácia's story of healing from a similar experience.

REEL TO REAL

1. Bobbi and Jesse home alone *(1:54)*

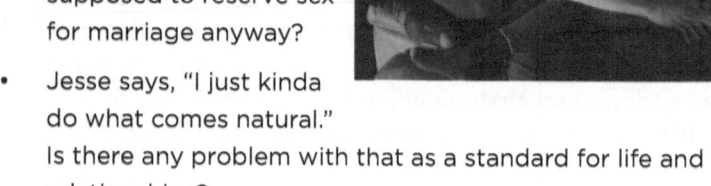

- What do you find most true-to-life about this scene?

- Why are Christians supposed to reserve sex for marriage anyway?

- Jesse says, "I just kinda do what comes natural." Is there any problem with that as a standard for life and relationships?

- Jesse also says a couple things that draw Bobbi back into making out: 1) he's unbelievably attracted to the most beautiful woman he knows; and 2) "You're making me believe, Bobbi. You're making me believe." Why do his words have that effect on her?

<u>LEADER</u>: The first scene had some humor in it. The next one doesn't.

2. At the tracks and afterward *(2:36)*

- "Oh God, what am I doing?" Bobbi says. Do you think young people plan to get into situations like this, or do they get there without really knowing where they're going?

- "I don't want you to feel any pressure. I just want you to know that I love you," Jesse says. Is he pressuring her or not?

- Imagine Bobbi's inner monologue as she sits in the car wondering what to do. What is she thinking?

- What are some words to describe the mood as Jesse drives Bobbi home and says goodnight? Why are they feeling this way?

- Twice in these scenes, Jesse tells Bobbi that he loves her. *Love* can mean many different things. What is Jesse trying to say?

LEADER: Sexuality is a powerful aspect of our being. God made it that way. Things that are powerful can be used for great good when used in accordance with God's design. And they can cause great harm when taken outside God's design.

After we come to appreciate the harm that careless sex can create—especially if we have learned this through personal

experience—there is one more important thing to understand: God is always waiting to bring us back to him. This is Grácia's experience, which she describes to Chase and OB by the island fireplace.

3. Grace tells her story *(2:10)*

- How did Grace end up in a negative relationship at her previous school?

- Did your opinion of Grace change once you heard her story? If so, in what way?

- Is it possible to live a lifestyle of purity again after one has done what Grace did? How does that happen?

- Grace says of God: "He loves Bobbi, he loves me, no matter what we've done." Do you believe that?

PRAYER

This may be an appropriate moment to lead the group in a few minutes of silent or guided reflection before God, to remember, consider, and receive his love for us no matter what we've done. Sensitivity is needed to shape the role confession may play in this prayer.

ENGAGE THE WORD

LEADER: Is Grace right? We should verify this in Scripture. Does God really love us no matter what? Can anyone point us to a verse? [Take suggestions.] **Here's one: "God demonstrates his own love for us in this: While we were still sinners, Christ died for us" (Romans 5:8). What an encouraging picture of God's love as expressed through the life of Jesus!**

Let's take a look at another scripture: John 8:1-11. Listen to this story with your eyes closed and imagine yourself being right there that day.

Read and discuss the account in John 8:1-11 of the woman caught in adultery.

Discuss

- Imagine being present at this scene. Which character do you most identify with?

- Does Jesus care that this woman committed adultery?

- In what way does he give her a fresh start in life?

- Have you ever experienced this kind of a fresh start in life? Do you need to experience it now?

REPORT FROM THE FRONTLINES

On the *Because of Grácia* Resources website, watch Louisa Wendorff, who plays the character of Josie in the film, talk about a Christian approach to physical attraction, purity in relationship, and fresh starts after failure. (Clip is 4:21.)

 ## CARRY IT OUT
Popularize Chastity

Break students into groups of 5 to adapt 1 Corinthians 6:18–20 into a popular musical genre. Remind your students to be creative and have fun. They can write a rap that quotes from the text, or rewrite the lyrics to a pop song to reflect a new set of values based on these verses. Challenge them to work as much of the scripture into their presentation as possible.

CONVERSATION 3
HOW DO YOU GROW IN TRUE FRIENDSHIP?
HEALTHY DATING 101

KEY INSIGHT

>>> Saving sex for marriage doesn't mean that young people shouldn't explore special relationships, it just means they should invest their time in building true friendship rather than in premature exploration of physical intimacy.

AT A GLANCE

SET THE STAGE
- Double Double
- Silent Interviews

REEL TO REAL
- Chase and Grace's first date
- Bobbi and Jesse at the bleachers
- Chase and Grace in her backyard

ENGAGE THE WORD
- Romans 11:33–12:3: Do not conform

INTERGENERATIONAL SIDEBAR
- Friendship and dating in the past

REPORT FROM THE FRONTLINES
- Chris Massoglia (Chase) and Moriah Peters (Grace) on healthy relating

CARRY IT OUT
- Having "That Conversation"
- A New Kind of Dating

PREP

REEL TO REAL / REPORT FROM THE FRONTLINES: Cue up the session's three movie clips and the video testimony for presentation.

ENGAGE THE WORD: Bookmark the session's main text (Romans 11:33–12:3).

INTERGENERATIONAL SIDEBAR: *Invite a guest to the session who can share stories of friendship and dating in the past.*

 SET THE STAGE

 Double Double

Have participants get into groups of 3 and take turns trying out this hand game in pairs. The directions for this activity are also available in their student guides.
    Chant the words and perform the actions at the same time, gradually getting faster as you go.

Actions
- *double*: bumping the soft sides of your fists with your partner's as though pounding on a door
- *this*: clapping your palms against your partner's
- *that*: clapping the backs of your palms against your partner's

Chant

double double this this
double double that that
double this double that
double double this that

See if the students can proceed faster and faster the more confident they become with the game.

2 Silent Interviews

Divide the group into pairs and give them the assignment of telling their partner 2 interesting things about themselves without speaking (using charades-style actions only). Switch actors after 2 minutes. When both partners have performed, ask everyone to introduce their partner to a nearby pair by sharing what they learned about him or her.

Discuss

- How are these two games like a healthy friendship?

REEL TO REAL

LEADER: The characteristics of healthy friendship that you have described apply to all kinds of friendship, including friendship with the same sex. But they especially apply to dating relationships, since those are uniquely vulnerable to drifting away from true friendship into something else. Let's take a look at some dating examples from the film and see how they measure up against these ideals.

1. Chase and Grace's first date *(2:40)*

- What's going on in this scene?

- Why does this situation begin so awkwardly for Chase? How does it get easier for him?

- Did you pick up any specific ideas on how to grow true friendship?

2. Bobbi and Jesse at the bleachers *(1:23)*

- How is this conversation different from the last one we saw?

- When a young couple spends a lot of time exploring their physical

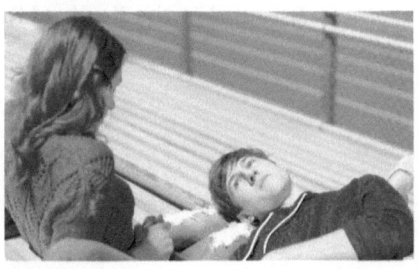

attraction to one another, what might happen to other aspects of the relationship?

- Based on this scene, do you have any additional ideas for growing true friendship?

3. Chase and Grace in her backyard *(2:32)*

- What was the problem with Grace's last dating relationship?

- What's your opinion of Chase and Grace's physical expressions of affection here: too much, not enough, or just right? What does the hand-holding and hug communicate?

- Which pattern of relationship do you see more of at your school: Chase and Grace's or Bobbi and Jesse's? How about in popular music, television, and movies?

<u>LEADER</u>: Scripture offers us some important guidance on this question of what patterns we should follow in life. A great example is found in the book of Romans.

ENGAGE THE WORD

Have a female member of the group read aloud Romans 11:33–12:2 and then, after a pause, have a male member do the same.

After 30 seconds of silence, ask the group to speak out, one by one, single words or phrases that lodged in their minds from the reading. Then discuss the following questions:

Discuss

- How do these words of the apostle Paul relate, either directly or indirectly, to the themes of friendship, love, and dating?

- What is "the pattern of this world" for relationships between guys and girls?

- What could it mean to "not conform to the pattern of this world" in this area of life?

 # PRAYER

Guide participants in a prayer for the Spirit of God to shape their relationships toward God-honoring purity and true, life-giving friendship.

INTERGENERATIONAL SIDEBAR

Give the floor to your invited guest for a few minutes to speak to the following questions:

- What was "the pattern of this world" for love and dating when you were a teenager?

- To what degree did you "not conform"? Were there any written or unwritten rules for Christians regarding love and dating?

- Is there anything you would do differently if you could have another chance at it? Do you have any special advice or encouragement to give young people today?

 ## REPORT FROM THE FRONTLINES

On the *Because of Grácia* Resources website, watch Chris Massoglia, who plays Chase in the film, and Moriah Peters, who plays Grace in the film, talk about developing a sense of purity grounded in the love of God. (Clips are 4:12 and 4:17.)

CARRY IT OUT

 Having "That Conversation"

Break class participants into small groups. Then present participants with a familiar scenario:

A young couple has realized that they are spending too much time, and going too far, in their expressions of physical affection. Ask your students to write a script of the imaginary conversation between the two as they discuss the issue and make a new plan for their relationship.

Variant: Participants can improvise a role-play of the situation on the spot.

A New Kind of Dating

Invite participants to create a short video promoting healthy and creative dating practices in a lighthearted way. They should begin by printing the words of Romans 12:2 ("Do not conform to the pattern of this world, but be transformed by the renewing of your mind") one by one on sheets of paper—one large word per page. Then they should choose a friend of the opposite sex and use a smartphone to record a video in which they display the words of the verse one page after the other. The idea is to create a brief, creative, thought-provoking, possibly funny scene of a date that is not "according to the pattern of this world" but that demonstrates a God-transformed way of thinking. Have students share videos with each other when time is almost up.

( ) FINAL REMARKS

As you end your group session, we recommend saving several minutes for final reflection. Give students an opportunity to ask questions and speak freely about the topics you've covered through this guide. Ask them to talk about what they've learned, how they've changed, and how they plan to move forward. Consider closing your session with another prayer of blessing over your students, asking God to be with them along the journey ahead.

ABOUT THE AUTHORS

CHRIS FRIESEN
Chris Friesen: A teacher and pastor by profession and a songwriter and storyteller on the side, Chris Friesen holds a master's degree in theology from Mennonite Brethren Biblical Seminary at Fresno Pacific University and has worked for years in youth, young adult, and children's ministry, from the Canadian boreal forest to the inner city. He resides in Saskatoon, Saskatchewan, on the Canadian prairies, where he makes music with his wife and six children in the Friesen Family Band.

MICHELLE SIMES
Michelle Simes is a Special Education teacher and homeschool mom who is married to Tom, the writer/ director of Because Of Gracia. She has written pro-life and youth curriculum material for schools and churches. Michelle has worked in ministry to teens and young adults around the areas of chastity and sanctity of life issues. She currently resides in the heartland of Canada, Saskatoon, Saskatchewan. Michelle and Tom have been blessed with thirty three years of marriage and four beautiful children ages 16-26.

COMING TO SELECT THEATERS **SEPTEMBER 2017**

BECAUSE of GRÁCIA

PLAN YOUR GROUP SCREENING TODAY!

Site licensing available.
Contact **info@becauseofgracia.com** for more information
or visit **http://www.becauseofgracia.com**

BECAUSE of GRÁCIA

PRODUCTS AND RESOURCES

BECAUSE OF GRÁCIA: A Novel

Based on the award-winning film.

ISBN: 978-1-947297-00-5
eBook: 978-1-947297-01-2

Abbreviated leader's guides for teaching individual themes

A Film and Faith Leader Guide: Theme 1 Practicing Friendship

ISBN: 978-1-947297-06-7
eBook: 978-1-947297-07-4

BECAUSE OF GRÁCIA: Student Guide
A Film and Faith Conversation Guide

Nine-session study guide based on three major themes of the award-winning film.

ISBN: 978-1-947297-02-9
eBook: 978-1-947297-03-6

A Film and Faith Leader Guide: Theme 2 Choosing Life

ISBN: 978-1-947297-08-1
eBook: 978-1-947297-09-8

A Film and Faith Leader Guide: Theme 3 Voicing Faith

ISBN: 978-1-947297-10-4
eBook: 978-1-947297-11-1

BECAUSE OF GRÁCIA: Curriculum Bundle

Includes the leader's guide, one student guide and DVD clips from the film.

ISBN: 978-1-947297-12-8

AVAILABLE WHEREVER BOOKS ARE SOLD
For ordering information, visit **dexteritycollective.co** or write to **info@dexteritycollective.co**.

www.ingramcontent.com/pod-product-compliance
Lightning Source LLC
Chambersburg PA
CBHW021452080526
44588CB00009B/816